LAUGHING MATTERS

GROSS-OUT JOKES

Compiled by Pam Rosenberg

Illustrated by Patrick Girouard

Special thanks to Katie Cottrell for her assistance in compiling source materials.

Published in the United States of America by The Child's World®
PO Box 326, Chanhassen, MN 55317-0326
800-599-READ
www.childsworld.com

Acknowledgments
The Child's World®: Mary Berendes, Publishing Director

Editorial Directions, Inc.: E. Russell Primm, Editorial Director and Line Editor; Katie Marsico, Assistant Editor; Matthew Messbarger, Editorial Assistant; Susan Ashley, Proofreader

The Design Lab: Kathleen Petelinsek, Designer; Kari Thornborough, Page Production

Library of Congress Cataloging-in-Publication Data
Rosenberg, Pam.
  Gross-out jokes / compiled by Pam Rosenberg ; illustrated by Patrick Girouard.
      p. cm. — (Laughing matters)
   ISBN 1-59296-280-7 (library bound : alk. paper) I. Riddles, Juvenile. 2. Wit and humor, Juvenile. I. Girouard, Patrick. II. Title. III. Series.
   PN6371.5.R576 2005
   818'.602—dc22   2004016861

DROP OR FALLING JOKES

What do you get when you drop a piano down a mine shaft?

A-flat minor.

What do you get when you pour boiling water down a rabbit hole?

Hot cross bunnies.

If at first you don't succeed, skydiving is definitely not your sport!

CANNIBAL JOKES

Two cannibals are eating a clown and one says, "Does this taste funny to you?"

Did you hear about the cannibal who was expelled from school? He was buttering up his teacher.

Why did the cannibal eat the tightrope walker? He wanted a balanced meal.

Little Cannibal: I hate my teacher.
Mother Cannibal: Then just eat your salad, dear.

What's a cannibal's favorite game?
Swallow the leader.

Have you heard about the new cannibal restaurant?
Dinner costs an arm and a leg.

What do cannibals eat for dessert?
Chocolate-covered aunts.

What do cannibals eat for breakfast?
Buttered host.

Thank You!

05321

TOTAL

6

What's the most important rule in chemistry?
Never lick the spoon.

Boy: Mom, all the kids at school say I'm a werewolf! Is that true?
Mom: No, of course not! Now be quiet and comb your face.

7

DOG JOKES

What do you call a dog with no legs? It doesn't matter, he won't come anyway.

Where do you find a no-legged dog? Right where you left him.

If H_2O is on the inside of a fire hydrant, what's on the outside? K9P.

8

What do you call a chicken that crosses the road without looking both ways? Dead.

UNTITLED JOKES

What happened after the cowboy drank eight Cokes? He burped 7-Up.

When is it good manners to spit in a cowboy's face? When his mustache is on fire.

SKUNK JOKES

What do you get if you cross a skunk and a boomerang?
A smell you can't get rid of.

What did the judge say when the skunk walked into the courtroom?
Odor in the court!

What would you get if you crossed a Martian, a skunk, and an owl?
An animal that stinks to high heaven and doesn't give a hoot.

EATING OUT JOKES

What do spiders like to order at fast-food restaurants?
Burgers and flies.

What does a lion eat when he goes to a restaurant?
The waiter.

What do you get when you eat onions and beans?
Tear gas.

11

SEASIDE JOKES

Why couldn't Batman
go fishing?
Because Robin ate
all the worms.

What do sharks
call swimmers?
Dinner.

Did you hear about the boy
who does bird impressions?
He eats worms.

BAIT

FOOD JOKES

How many rotten eggs does it take to make a stink bomb?

A phew.

Is it proper to eat a hamburger with your fingers?

No, you should eat your fingers separately.

What's the difference between roast beef and pea soup?

Anybody can roast beef.

NOSE JOKES

If a cow laughs, does milk come out of its nose?

What's green and hangs from trees? Giraffe snot.

What's the difference between boogers and broccoli? Kids won't eat broccoli.

How do you make a tissue dance? Put a little boogey in it.

Why do gorillas have large nostrils? Because they have big fingers.

15

BACKSIDE JOKES

Why was the sand wet?
  Because the sea-weed.

Why did the toilet paper roll down the hill?
  It wanted to get to the bottom.

Did you hear about the skunk who went to church?
  He had his own pew.

What's the last thing that goes through a bug's mind as it hits the windshield?
  Its rear.

What should you take before every meal?
  A seat.

What would you call a phone in a bathroom?
A smellular phone.

Which college has the most bathrooms?
P.U.

What do you get when you eat a prune pizza?
Pizzeria.

Why did the boy bring toilet paper to the birthday party?
He was a party pooper.

What nationality are you when you go to the bathroom?
European.

Did you hear the joke about the skunk?
You don't want to— it stinks.

Student: Teacher, can I go to the bathroom?
Teacher: In a couple of minutes. You need to say your alphabet first.
Student: OK. ABCDEFGHIJKLMNOQRSTUVWXYZ.
Teacher: Very good, but where's the P?
Student: Running down my leg.

MISSING BODY PARTS JOKES

What do you call a cow with no legs?
Ground beef.

What do you call a man with no arms and no legs who's on the wall?
Art.

What do you call a man with no arms and no legs who's in the water?
Bob.

What do you call a man with no arms and no legs who's on the floor?
Matt.

A man was working with an electric saw when he accidentally sawed off all 10 fingers. He quickly rushed to the emergency room. The doctor there said, "Give me the fingers and I'll see what I can do." "But I don't have the fingers!" the man said. "What? You don't have the fingers?" said the doctor. "You should have brought them to me. We have all kinds of operations. We could have done microsurgery and put them back as good as new." "But Doc," the man said, "I couldn't pick them up!"

MUTILATING JOKES

What happened when the scientist fell into the lens-grinding machine?
He made a spectacle of himself.

What do you get when you run over a parakeet with a lawn mower?
Shredded tweet.

What's green and red and goes 50 miles per hour?
A frog in a blender.

What did the butcher say when he backed into the meat grinder?
Looks like I'm getting a little behind in my work.

About Patrick Girouard:

Patrick Girouard has been illustrating books for almost 15 years but still looks remarkably lifelike. He loves reading, movies, coffee, robots, a beautiful red-haired lady named Rita, and especially his sons, Marc and Max. Here's an interesting fact: A dog named Sam lives under his drawing board. You can visit him (Patrick, not Sam) at www.pgirouard.com.

About Pam Rosenberg:

Pam Rosenberg is a former junior high school teacher and corporate trainer. She currently works as an author, editor, and the mother of Sarah and Jake. She took on this project as a service to all her fellow parents of young children. At least now their kids will have lots of jokes to choose from when looking for the one they will tell their parents over and over and over again!